40
STRONG

A TACTICAL GUIDE FOR BECOMING A **MAN OF GOD**

40 STRONG: A Tactical Guide for Becoming a Man of God
Copyright © 2025 by Jerrell Jobe
ISBN: 979-8-9921087-3-6

Printed in the United States of America.

40 STRONG is about **7 practices**, done with a **crew of at least 4 people**, over the course of **40 days**. Is it a challenge? Sure, if you're up for it. But, more than that, it's an invitation to a new way of living. A way of connecting with God throughout the day, experiencing life in community, and knowing the on-going power of life transformation - mind, body and spirit.

The Journey is the Destination,

Jerrell Jobe

THE 7 PRACTICES

These 7 core practices are strategic in helping you connect with God and others throughout the day. Seven may seem a little daunting, but they're actually quite doable. In fact, all seven practices can be completed in about 40-minutes total, a few minutes at a time throughout the day. (Okay, more-or-less, but there's just something about the number 40.) Each day after you complete each item, simply put a ☑ next to each of the 7 icons on the right side of each day's content.

PRAYER OF COMMITMENT

The first decision every day is an act of surrender. Each morning, we begin by committing the day and ourselves to God. This simple prayer sets the course and direction for everything we will do each day. It goes like this: "Today is Yours God. Today, I am Yours. Today, lead me, guide me and prompt me by Your Spirit. Today, I desire to follow and obey You. Amen."

2  PUSH-UPS / SIT-UPS

Are any instructions really needed here? Kneel down and knock it out. Do 4 push-ups. Then on your back and execute 4 mighty crunches. Let out a grunt if it helps fire you up.

3  READ SCRIPTURE

The Bible is fuel for the soul. Without it we are famished. Portions of the Bible have been carefully selected for this journey. Each day will give you a reference to read. Open a Bible and dig in, it will only take about 4-minutes.

REFLECT & PRAY

Reading is only part of the experience. Turn the daily reading into a prayerful conversation with God, reflection with others, and action steps for living. You'll be amazed at how much God will say to you, when you set aside time to listen, even if it's only 4-minutes a day.

PRAY FOR YOUR CREW

40 STRONG is meant to be done in the context of a community of at least 4 people, referred to as your crew. Each day, you will pray for your crew members. Give it just 4-minutes. Surely, through your daily texting, phone calls, and weekly connecting times, you will have plenty to pray about. However, if you're still struggling with what to pray for, you can find some ideas to get you started in the Tactical Resources, located in the back of this guide.

MOVE

It's one thing to love Jesus with your mind, time, and resources. But, loving Jesus also includes your whole body. Ultimately, love is an action. We want to love God with our whole being. Taking care of our physical bodies enables us to do the stuff God wants us to do. So, at some point everyday, get up and get moving for 20-minutes. Go to the gym, walk, run, bike, swim, or chase a duck, it doesn't matter. Just get up and get moving.

PRAYING BACKWARDS

The day starts with a Prayer of Commitment. The day ends with a How'd it go? You could call this a prayer of examen. For about 4-minutes, you will journey back through your day with God. You will ask the Spirit of God to speak to you, and show you how the day went from His perspective. There's a helpful guide to do this in the Tactical Resources, located in the back.

THE JOURNEY BEGINS

READ Genesis 12:1-9; Hebrews 11:8-10

REFLECT

God told Abram that "all the peoples on earth" would be blessed through him (v.2-3). However, in order for this to happen, Abram had to leave (v.1). Abram had to embark on a journey of faith. So must we...

Where does God tell Abram he is going? (see last part of v.1)

Did Abram know where he was going?

How did he respond? (Genesis 12:4 and last part of Hebrews 11:8)

Do you find it challenging to obey God if you don't know all the details ahead of time?

PRAYER

Take a moment and commit the next 40 days to God. Like Abram, we are embarking on a life changing faith journey. We don't know all that will transpire, or what will be required of us, but we commit these 40 days to God, and trust that we will be transformed in the process.

Want to take this to the next level? Sign your name on the line below. Want to add a little extra to that? Don't go it alone, have your crew members sign your book as well, as a way of committing to journeying with one another and God over the next 40 days.

_____

SIGN HERE

IN MOTION

2

READ Daniel 1:1-21; Daniel 6:1-28

REFLECT

In both of these scenarios, Daniel and his friends faced a tremendous challenge. Yet, rather than compromise, they were able to stand strong. Their strength was discovered on the day of battle. But, it was cultivated in the previous weeks and months that preceded in private.

What does it say Daniel did? (Daniel 1:8)

What does the word "resolve" mean?

See also the last part of Daniel 6:10. Write out the last part of that verse.

40 STRONG is about "resolve." It's about intentionally engaging in a few habits every day.

What was the result of Daniel's resolve and discipline? (Daniel 1:20; 6:10)

ACTION

On a scale of 0 to 10, 0 being very low and 10 being very high, how well do you do in following through and being consistent?

0 -------   ----- 5 -------   ------- 10
(Subject to Laziness)   (Do What's Needed)   (Live in Beast Mode All the Time)

Share with your crew what number you selected and why.

THE POWER OF THE OTHER

READ Ecclesiastes 4:9-12; Proverbs 17:17; Exodus 17:8-16

REFLECT

Exodus 17:8-16 is a fascinating story. Joshua is on the ground fighting. Moses has his arms raised in the air. Both are essential, the "doing" and the "praying." They work together. But, there's another component that's often overlooked. The power of someone standing beside you when you are weary in the battle.

What are some practical ways we can lift up the arms of another?

Over 40 STRONG, your crew is going to be like Aaron and Hur to you. They are going to help "lift up your arms." And, you are going to do the same for them.

ACTION

Send an encouraging text message to your crew.

DESERT PIRATES

READ Deuteronomy 25:17-19

REFLECT

The Amalekites were nomadic tribes of people in the Sinai and Negev desert. They were the pirates of the desert.

What was their tactic of attack? (Deuteronomy 25:18)

How might the Enemy of our souls operate in a similar manner?

What are the warning signs of someone who is "weary, worn out," and isolated from others?

ACTION

Share with your crew what your "warning signs" look like. Give them permission to speak into this area of your life.

HEALTHY RHYTHMS

READ Luke 5:12-16

REFLECT

How does Luke describe the ministry of Jesus? (Luke 5:15)

Jesus' ministry schedule was full. As news spread about Him, more and more people pushed and clamored for His attention. Yet, what does it say Jesus "often" did? (Luke 5:16)

Jesus demonstrates for us what healthy rhythms of work, ministry, and life look like. Like Jesus, we must intentionally break from the busyness of life and simply be with God. We need to pray, breathe, sit in silence, and be replenished.

If Jesus needed to "withdraw" from the chaos and spend time alone with God, how much more do we?

How are your current "rhythms" of life?

What are some ways you can "withdraw" throughout your day, and pray? (Even if it's for only 2-4 minutes)

ACTION

Write down a few ideas of when and how you can do this. Give it a try today.

LESSONS IN THE WILDERNESS

READ Exodus 16:1-36; 17:1-7

REFLECT

The wilderness is a place of testing and training. It is during these difficult seasons that we are challenged in our faith and devotion. But, if we are willing, it is during these same times that we are forged and trained into the people God is calling us to be.

As you read through chapters 16 and 17 of Exodus, what lessons was God teaching the children of Israel? (You may find it helpful to read back through these passages.)

Currently, what do you sense God is trying to teach you?

ACTION

Today, share and compare your observations with your crew.

100 BLESSINGS A DAY

READ Psalm 103:1-22

REFLECT

During the time of Jesus, there was a tradition called, "100 Blessings a Day." Prayers were developed for virtually every occasion and moment throughout one's day. The goal was to develop an on-going, uninterrupted, conversation with God, saturated with an ever-present awareness of God's provision, activity and goodness to us.

Reread Psalm 103. How many different things does the psalmist list? Try and count them.

ACTION

Compare the number you get with your to crew.

Make your own list of all the ways God has provided, is active, and has shown His goodness to you.

As you go through your day, give thanks to God.

THE PROMISE KEEPER

READ Genesis 28:10-22

REFLECT

Up to this point, Jacob has swindled his brother out of his birthright and deceived his father for his blessing. He's now on the run, under the guise of looking for a wife. Yet, even in the midst of these circumstances, God pursues Jacob and reveals Himself in a personal way. In fact, God makes 8 promises to Jacob.

What are these 8 promises? (v.13-15)

Which of these promises sticks out to you personally?

Do you sense God speaking one of these promises to you?
(If so, which one?)

ACTION

Write down and pray about the promise(s) that stuck out
to you personally.

ALTAR'D STATE

READ Genesis 28:10-22
(yes, we're reading it again today)

REFLECT

Jacob has a life altering encounter with God.

What did Jacob do to help him remember his encounter with God? (v.18–22)

What have been some of your life altering encounters with God?

ACTION

Share one of these encounters with your crew today.

A PLACE CALLED BETHEL

READ Genesis 28:10-22
(yes, we're reading it
again today)

REFLECT

Jacob sets out on roughly a 650 mile journey. After about 3-days of walking, he stops for the night, lays down and goes to sleep. While resting, he has a dream. This is a powerful encounter with God. Jacob even renames the place, Bethel. Literally, "House of God."

After waking up, Jacob is overcome with a sense of awe. Could he still tangibly feel the presence of God? Interestingly, upon reflection, Jacob says, "Surely the LORD is in the place, and I was not aware of it." (v.16)

Could it be, at times, God is active in our lives and circumstances, and like Jacob, we are "not aware of it"?

PRAYER

Ask God to help you become more "aware" of His presence and activity in your life, and throughout each day.

Pray for your crew and your family members, that God will help them to become more "aware" of His present nearness as well.

SEEING THE ONE WHO SEES ME

READ Genesis 16:1-14

11

REFLECT

Hagar, the Egyptian slave, has run away after being mistreated by Sarai. She desperately flees through the arid desert toward Egypt. She is weary, confused, and pregnant.

Go back and read verse 7.

This is a powerful phrase! "The angel of the LORD found Hagar."

God pursued and found her. God spoke to her, even called her by her very name.

Deeply moved by this encounter, Hagar declares, "You are the God who sees me. I have now seen the One who sees me."

God knows where you are in life. He sees what's going on in our lives. God sees even into the depths of our hearts and minds. It is here that He speaks to us.

PRAYER

God, I thank you that you know everything about me. Is there anything you want to say to me today...?

TWO QUESTIONS FOR THE JOURNEY

READ Genesis 16:1-14
(There is still more in this passage.)

REFLECT

Look back at verse 8. What does the angel ask Hagar?

At first glance, these seem like strange questions. We know that God knows where she's coming from and the direction she's currently headed. God knows the ridicule she's endured and the fear-filled pain piercing her soul. Nonetheless, God probes her with these two questions.

What if God is asking you the same two questions, how would you answer?

12

Where have you come from...?

Where are you going...?

ACTION

Write down a few sentences that summarize your answers.

At some point today, ask a friend, acquaintance, or co-worker these two questions and see where the conversation goes...

GOD IS AT WORK

READ Philippians 1:1-11; Philippians 2:12-13

13

REFLECT

Reread verse Philippians 1:6 and 2:13.

These verses affirm a central truth of our spiritual journey with Christ. It is God who "began" a "good work" within us. God is currently "at work within us." And, He will continue working until His purpose is accomplished.

Regardless of how vibrant or stagnant your "walk with God" may seem, know this, God is at work within your life. Even in difficult circumstances, stress-filled situations, or tense relationships. God is at work within us. And, we are, you could say, "under construction."

PRAYER

Ask God to show you how He has been working in your life and circumstances.

Write down a few of your observations.

OVERFLOW

READ Galatians 5:1-2; 5:13-25

14

REFLECT

What does Paul state Christ came to do?
(Galatians 5:1 and 13)

The Apostle Paul outlines two life sources that we will live from, the flesh or the Spirit. (Reread Galatians 5:16-18)

What are "acts of the flesh"? (Galatians 5:19-21)

What are some of the internal and external signs that we are living by the Spirit? (Galatians 5:22-23)

ACTION

Galatians 5 simply gives us a few things that help us to identify which life source we are living from. They are the byproduct, or rather overflow from what's going on within us. May we become people who consistently demonstrate the "fruit of the Spirit," in every arena of our lives. Pay close attention to your emotions and responses to others throughout the day. Ask God to show you when your present overflow isn't symptomatic of the "fruit of the Spirit" listed in v.22-23.

THE FRIEND EVERYBODY NEEDS

READ 1 Samuel 18:1-4; 19:1-12; 20:1-42

15

REFLECT

David and Jonathan had a loyal friendship. Scripture says they made a "covenant" with each other. In other words, they made a commitment to one another. In our culture we say, "I've got your back... I'm not going anywhere... I'm here for you..." Humans have been designed by God for community, for friendships. Many of us "know" people, but few of us are really "known" by anyone. A spiritual friend is someone who truly knows us, the good, the bad, and the ugly. They know the worst, and yet still see the best. We need people like this. 40 STRONG is about intentionally creating and developing these kinds of friendships.

ACTION

Thank God for those He's placed in your life, specifically those you would call close friends, even spiritual friends. Take a few moments and pray for them by name. Send them a message of what you're praying for them today.

A person without a soul friend is like a body without a head.
-Ancient Celtic Saying

INTO-ME-SEE

READ Ecclesiastes 4:9-12; Proverbs 17:17

16

REFLECT

The key to godly friendships that propel us further toward the people God is shaping us to be is fearlessness. Fear keeps most of us bound, silent, and reluctant to share "what's really going on." So often, it's said, "If they really knew this about me, they would treat me differently." Transformation happens through authentic transparency. Deep change emerges as we are willing to take a risk, "go there," and share with our crew what's really going on inside. It's been said, you can define the word "intimacy," by saying, "into me see." True friendship, takes off the masks, turns on the lights, and invites another person into our lives. Is there anything you've wanted to share with your crew, but have been afraid to do so? Take a step.

ACTION

If you've been holding back and are reluctant to share something with your crew, take a chance today, go there, take a step... If nothing comes to mind, share something with your crew about yourself that they don't know.

HOLDING NOTHING BACK

READ Jeremiah 38:14

17

REFLECT

While the context from the passage is multi-layered, v.14 offers some challenging advice for how we interact with those God has placed close to us. King Zedekiah said, "I am going to ask you something." There is power in questions. Zedekiah continues, "do not hide anything from me." In other words, don't hold anything back. Tell me what God says. Speak up and say what I need to hear.

What if we did that with those in our crew? To ask them a question about ourselves, extending to them permission to mirror back to us what they see in us. To be honest with us. For example: What if we said, "Is there anything you see in me that is counterproductive to the person God is calling me to be? Do you see anything in me that's hurting me?

If you were driving with a friend and someone was about to hit you, but you didn't see them coming your way, you'd want your friend to give a shout and alert you. The warning could save both of your lives. The passenger saw something the driver couldn't see, but when he became aware of it, they were better off because of it.

Life is like that at times. In our life, soul, or a relationship, we're about to swerve off the road and hit a ditch. What if our crew saw it and spoke up? These words are often challenging to hear, but they could save our lives.

ACTION

Ask your crew what they see in you. Give them permission to let you know when they see an area of your life or soul swerving.

CULTIVATING CURIOSITY

READ Luke 2:41-51

18

REFLECT

What did they find Jesus doing in the Temple? (v.46)

Studies show that a child asks 200-300 questions each day. The average adult asks 6. Somewhere along the way humans lose their curiosity and intrigue. Along with that, we are often prone to lose our sense of wonder and awe of creation and people.

Questions help remind us that we don't know everything. Questions are powerful. They unlock potential. Questions help to identify where God is at work and where change has been transpiring. Questions are essential to transformation.

ACTION

As you read the Bible, ask questions.

Start with: Who's speaking? Who are they talking to? Where is this taking place? When does this happen? What is God saying to me through this?

THE ART OF ASKING QUESTIONS

READ Luke 2:41-51
(Digging deeper)

19

REFLECT

The practice of asking questions is demonstrated throughout all of Jesus' life. In the first gospel written, the gospel of Mark, there are 67 accounts in which there is some sort of conversation. Within these 67 verbal exchanges, Jesus asks at least 50 questions. What would it look like for us to practice the art of asking questions to others?

ACTION

Here are a few ideas to get you started with your crew, as well as others you encounter along the way.

· What has stuck out to you in this week's readings?

· What else have you been reading?

· Which of the daily rhythms have been most exciting, life-giving, or challenging for you?

· What has Jesus been speaking to you lately?

· How do you feel like you've grown since we started 40 STRONG?

· How are things with you and God... Your spouse... Your children... Your work... etc...?

· What are you most passionate about right now?

AM I LISTENING?

READ Job 33:14-18; 1 Samuel 3:1-4:1

20

REFLECT

Who's voice did Samuel hear? (1 Samuel 3:4, 6, 8, 10)

Whose voice did Samuel think that he heard? (1 Samuel 3:5, 6, 8)

Could it be that at times, God is speaking to us as well, only we do not recognize His voice?

The spiritual practice of listening is an essential discipline that many of us overlook.

PRAYER

Take a few moments and pray through these questions (especially as each relates to your stage of life).

Listen and write down what you sense God is saying to you.

God is there anything you want to say to me regarding my...
...relationship with You?
...relationship with my spouse?
...relationship with my children and/or parents?
...relationship with my co-workers?
...relationship with the world around me?

ACTION

Share with your crew something that you sense God is speaking to you today.

AM I GROWING?

READ Colossians 1:9-11

21

REFLECT

One of the things Paul prays for us, is that we would always be "growing in the knowledge of God." Sometimes, it's hard to see how we are growing.

A student-disciple was discouraged about his perceived lack of growth. He expressed to his rabbi, "I just don't feel like I'm any different today than I was last year." His rabbi responded, "Last spring the trees were green. Now, in the fall, they are brilliant orange, yellow and red. Yet, no one saw them change..."

PRAYER

"God, I believe that I am growing and changing. Help me to see how."

COMPARISON KILLS

READ 1 Samuel 8:1-22

REFLECT

What did the people want? (1 Samuel 8:5)

What was their motivation? (1 Samuel 8:20)

God had called the people of Israel to be "set apart" and different from "all the other nations." In fact, Israel was supposed to demonstrate what it looked like to follow God. Instead, they desired to be like those around them.

PRAYER

God, show me any area where I'm comparing myself to those around me. Show me any way I'm thinking like the Israelites, believing that things would be better, if only I _____ .

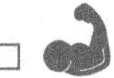

ACTION

Share with your crew what God shows you.

A NEW HEART

READ 1 Samuel 9:1-27; 10:1-27

REFLECT

What stuck out to me in this passage?

What questions do I have?

What do I sense God saying to me?

ACTION

Compare your reflections with your crew.

A KINGDOM LOST

READ 1 Samuel 13:1-15; 1 Samuel 15:1-35

24

REFLECT

What did the Amalekites do to Israel?
(see 1 Samuel 15:2; Deuteronomy 25:17-19)

What do 1 Samuel chapter 13 and 15 have in common? In both cases, what did Saul do, or rather not do?

What stuck out to me in this passage? What questions do I have? What do I sense God saying to me?

PRAYER

God, is there an arena of my life that I have not fully surrendered to You? Is there an area of my life that I am not being obedient to You and Your Word? I want to be fully devoted to You, holding nothing back.

WHAT DO YOU SEE?

READ 1 Samuel 9:2; 10:23-24; 16:1-13;
2 Corinthians 5:16

REFLECT

How does Scripture describe Saul? (1 Samuel 9:2 and 10:23-24)

What mistake did Samuel make when he "saw" Eliab? (1 Samuel 16:6)

Reread 1 Samuel 16:7. What does this verse tell us about God?

Our culture is fixated with outward looks. Appearance is everything. The Bible teaches us something about God. People are more than their outward appearances. Further, people are more than their houses, cars, and bank accounts. What would happen if we began to see people the way God sees them? What if we treated people the way God sees them? What would this look like practically?

PRAYER

God, may Your Spirit convict me when I pay more attention to how things look and appear on the outside, than who people are on the inside.

A HEART AFTER GOD

READ Acts 13:22; 1 Samuel 13:14; 16:1-13

26

REFLECT

Why did God say he chose David to be king?

What does it mean to have "a heart after God"?

ACTION

With your crew, come up with ten things that describe "a heart after God."

VALLEY OF ELAH

READ 1 Samuel 17:1-52

27

REFLECT

What stuck out to me in this passage?

What questions do I have?

What do I sense God saying to me?

ACTION

Compare your reflections with your crew.

GIANTS IN THE LAND

READ 1 Samuel 17:1-52
(Let's read it again)

28

REFLECT

Daily, the giant Goliath, taunted God's people. He instilled fear.
They were paralyzed on the battlefield. There are still giants in the
land. They instill fear and paralyze us from living out our purpose
with passion.

PRAYER

God, show me any "giants" in my life....

ACTION

Share with your crew any "giants" that God brought to your attention.

CARRY THE CHEESE

READ 1 Samuel 17:1-52
(Read it again. There's more to see)

REFLECT

What did David's father Jesse ask David to do? (1 Samuel 17:17-18)

The story begins with David simply carrying some bread and cheese to his brothers. The story ends with David carrying the head of the giant off the battlefield.

Consider this: David's faithfulness in the small, menial tasks of life prepared him to be a giant slayer. The same is true for us. It's our faithfulness in the small, routine, seemingly insignificant moments of life that prepare us to fulfill God's purposes for our life.

Everyone wants to be a giant killer, but few are willing to carry the cheese. But, it is as we are willing to carry the cheese that we are postured to slay the giants in our world.

PRAYER

God, today, wherever I find myself, help me to be willing to simply "carry the cheese." No matter how menial the task, may I do everything I do today, as if I'm doing it for You.

LOOKOUT BELOW

READ 2 Samuel 11:1-17

30

REFLECT

In the spring, kings go to battle. For some reason, David stayed at home. Things go downhill from there. Lust leads to a one night stand. Pregnancy leads to cover-up, and ultimately murder. It's been said that, "Sin will take you farther than you want to go, keep you longer than you want to stay, and cost you more than you want to pay."

PRAYER

God, like David, is there something I'm supposed to be doing, but I'm not?

God, like David, are there any "rooftops" I've been lingering on?

God, have I allowed my eyes, heart, or emotions to become attached to another person in a manner that is unholy?

ACTION

Set up a time to meet in person or have a phone call with your crew. Have an honest conversation about anything God spoke to you about. Be willing to ask each other candid questions. More importantly, be willing to answer honestly.

PERSPECTIVE FROM PRISON

31

READ Philippians 1:1-30

REFLECT

What stuck out to me from this chapter?

How does Paul's perspective, of his circumstances and life, challenge or encourage you today in your life and circumstances?

PRAYER

Take a few moments and pray Philippians 1:9-11 as a personalized prayer for each person in your crew.

CHOOSING HUMILITY

READ Philippians 2:1-30

32

REFLECT

Jesus, though being in very nature God, did not push his weight around. He came to serve others. He is the ultimate example of humility. And, we are encouraged to live our lives in a similar manner. Paul gives us a few examples of what this begins to look like in practice (Philippians 2:2-4).

ACTION

"In your relationships with one another, have the same mindset as Christ Jesus." As you go through your day, seek to value others, looking to their interests, and honoring them both with your words and actions.

GOD CHASER

READ Philippians 3:1-21

33

REFLECT

What stuck out to me from this chapter?

What do me hear God saying to me today?

ACTION

Is there any action required based on what God is saying to you? Text your crew the verse that stuck out to you the most from Philippians chapter 3. Share with them why.

LEARNING TO REJOICE

READ Philippians 4:1-23

34

REFLECT

What stuck out to me from this chapter?

What do I hear God saying to me today?

ACTION

Slowly reread Philippians 4:4-9 out loud.

WISDOM FOR THE ASKING

READ James 1:1-27

35

REFLECT

James chapter one focuses on two big ideas: a) finding God's perspective and wisdom in the midst of difficult circumstances, trials and temptation (James 1:2-18); and b) the power accessible to us when God's Word is integrated into our lives (James 1:19-27).

Which of these big ideas spoke to me the most today?

What is God saying to me through this passage?

ACTION

What do I hear God telling me to do today? "Today, I want you to _____."

PLAYING FAVORITES

READ James 2:1-26

36

REFLECT

On Day 25, we were challenged to see and treat people the way God sees them. James chapter 2 reminds us of this same truth. James adds that as followers of Jesus, we "must not show favoritism" to people based on their perceived status, appearance, or level of importance.

James uses the example of giving preferential treatment to the rich, in other words, those who can do something for me. Do you treat people differently based on their status, economic status, or appearance?

What is God saying to me through this passage?

ACTION

What do I hear God telling me to do today? "Today, I want you to_____."

BITS, RUDDERS & FOREST

READ Proverbs 18:21; James 3:1-18

37

REFLECT

James uses some powerful images of ship rudders, horse bits, and a small spark igniting a forest fire to describe the power of the tongue. Our words can heal or wound; build up or destroy. At times, we can fall into a pattern of communicating with others that is more destructive than wholesome.

Are there patterns of communication with our spouse, children, or co-workers that have become "normal," but may not be "healthy?"

Are there any patterns of communication, or ways of speaking to those around you that need some adjustment?

ACTION

What do I hear God telling me to do today?
"Today, I want you to_____."

Share with you crew what you sense God is saying to you.

SELFISHNESS OR SUBMISSION

READ James 4:1-17

38

REFLECT

James makes a poignant observation: external arguments almost always emerge out of internal selfishness. When we don't get our way, or our expectations aren't met, we lash out and punish others with our words and actions, or through silence and withdrawal. The antidote to selfishness is submission to God. Jesus modeled this well, when He said to the Father-God, "Not my will, but yours be done."

What is God saying to me through this passage?

ACTION

What do I hear God telling me to do today? "Today, I want you to_____."

If you trust yourself you will need yourself to sustain yourself, but if you trust the Lord the Lord takes full responsibility of sustaining you.
-Shadrack T. Ashaiyo

BE PATIENT & STAND FIRM

READ James 5:1-12

39

REFLECT

James reminds us to stand firm, be patient, and persevere in life, because after all, God is compassionate, merciful, and near. The ground may look barren today, but there are seeds germinating underneath the surface. In time, they will sprout, bloom, and provide a harvest.

Is there an area of your life where you've yet to see the "promise" fulfilled? A situation, or relationship that is still struggling, in need of a breakthrough? James encourages us to hold on and not give up. We are told to "be patient and stand firm, because the Lord's coming is near."

What stuck out to me in this passage? Is there a situation where I've lost hope, become discouraged, and began to give up?

ACTION

Share with your crew what stuck out to you today. Pray for one another, based on each person's reflection of the passage and what God is saying.

A MAN LIKE US

READ James 5:13-20

REFLECT

Elijah was a prophet, who lived during the 9th century BC. This was a dark time for the nation of Israel. Yet, it was during these dark times, that God used Elijah to speak truth to the people, and to demonstrate God's power. Before we regulate Elijah to the Hall of Fame and far removed from our own reach, James reminds us of an important truth, "Elijah was a human being, even as we are." At times, Elijah experienced bouts of depression and struggled to see things from God's perspective. Yet, we are told, "he prayed," and God answered. He was a conduit of God's supernatural power. James uses this example to teach us that "the prayer of a righteous person is powerful and effective."

As we wrap up this 40 day journey, like Elijah, we may not be perfect, but we are different. We may not have yet arrived, but we are changing. We are further down the path, but we have not reached our destination. The journey is the destination. Walking with God throughout the day is the goal. To become more aware of God's present nearness is our aim. And, as we connect with God in the midst of our everyday routines, we will continue to be transformed into the image of His Son and make a difference in the world in which we live.

ACTION

Set up a time to meet with your crew in person. Share how you have grown through 40 STRONG. What are your next steps as an individual? What are your next steps together as a crew?

PRAYER OF COMMITMENT
- Today is Yours God.
- Today, I am Yours.
- Today, lead me, guide me, and prompt me by Your Spirit.
- Today, I desire to follow and obey You.

PRAYING BACKWARDS

Invitation.
Pause. Breath. God, I thank you that You are with me and You love me as I am. You know everything about me. I pray that You would shine Your light on my day and help me to see it as You do.

Gratitude.
God, the day I have just lived is a gift from You. I choose to be grateful for it. (Look back through your day hour-by-hour, place-by-place, person-by-person and begin to give thanks for each of the gifts you received.)

Review.
Spirit of God, guide me through the day I just completed. (As you go through your day, hour-by-hour, place-by-place, person-by-person, be attentive to what God is showing you.)

Forgiveness.
As God identifies sin(s), actions, attitudes, responses, even ways of thinking and feeling that emerged throughout your day, bring them before God. Confess them for what they are. Ask for forgiveness and grace.

Renewal.
God, I don't know all that tomorrow will bring, but You do. Help me to be aware of how You are with me. Guide me. Grant me the grace needed for every encounter I face and person I meet along the way... Amen.

PRAYING FOR OTHERS

Ephesians 6:18-19, And pray in the Spirit on all occasions with all kinds of prayers and requests. With this in mind, be alert and always keep on praying for all the Lord's people. Pray also for me...

The following are few ideas to get you started when you don't know how you should pray for others:
1. For a greater awareness of God's Presence and activity in their lives.
2. For an increased passion and intimacy with God.
3. For a fresh desire to engage God through Scripture & prayer.
4. For their family (marriage, spouse and children, if applicable).
5. To fully utilize their God-given gifts and abilities at church, work and community.

Philippians 1:19, for I know that through your prayers and God's provision of the Spirit of Jesus Christ what has happened to me will turn out for my deliverance.

www.ingramcontent.com/pod-product-compliance
Lightning Source LLC
Chambersburg PA
CBHW082227140626
46556CB00020B/3377